BETTER THAN WEALTH TAX

By

Indraneel Das, Ph.D.

NOVEMBER 2019

*This book is dedicated to
the Late Prof. Russell T. Blackwood,
Prof. Emeritus, Hamilton College,
for always standing by me,
and to Columbia University
for my first serious education
on how capital works.*

Table Of Contents

Introduction

T hank you for buying this book – I'll do my best to get you thinking, if not more.

By now, whether you are a morning commuter, a freelancer, or a business owner, you have probably seen a few headlines on "a wealth tax in America". The topic has sparked off a variety of debate.

To clarify my position, I am not writing this book because there is even a remote possibility of me facing a wealth tax. Neither do I have any affiliation with any political party or special interest group. My (ambitious) goal, as a thinking citizen of the United States, is simply to reconcile conflicting needs of various parties and propose a better way. Somewhat by coincidence, I happen to be at a point where I did not have to seek anyone's approval or clearance to publish this book. You probably guessed - no one's paying me to write this book either.

My degrees are not in Economics, I am mostly self-taught – so I hope economists will pardon my 'alternate terminology' and see the concepts behind them. I have a Ph.D. in Computational & Applied Mathematics, specializing in Operations Research, and an MBA in Finance. I have worked with many corporate executives, analysts, scientists and engineers – but never with economists. I hope therein lies the possibility of a fresh perspective.

In my earlier days at a US corporation, I came up with methods for performing certain safety-critical computations in milliseconds (thankfully, the US Patent & Trademarks Office found them reasonable). These days I spend most of my time looking for investment ideas and themes. I started thinking about the wealth tax debate, and gradually a motley of thoughts crystallized and fell in place – that was the genesis of this book.

More than two decades ago I wrote a Ph.D. thesis on *non-linear multi-criteria optimization* – classically known as Pareto optimality, but for nonlinear problems. How does one find alternatives that best balance the needs of multiple conflicting parties? That perspective, perhaps, is the fundamental angle of this proposition.

This book is being written with the United States of America in mind. But it could very well apply to another nation. However, unless the whole world were to converge under some utopian, quasi-homogeneous political, economic and 'border-free' coalition, "global wealth inequality" is outside the scope of this treatise.

This book is only a starting point. The goal is to communicate a self-contained set of thoughts and ideas within the reader's attention span – hence brevity was a focus. If a dozen thinkers and personalities in positions of action take up and echo these ideas, I would consider the work a success. If this reaches the level of readership/citation that my Ph.D. work from 1997 has, I would be blown away. If I am called into follow-up discussions and further work, I would be humbled and be on my way.

Wealth tax- what and why?

What is wealth tax? An owner of a piece of real estate pays a percentage of the assessed value of the property as a 'property tax' each year. A wealth tax would apply to the value of all assets, not just real estate. Such assets would include cash, stocks, bonds sitting in brokerage accounts, as well as stakes in private companies, software ventures, laundromats and delis. Several countries in Europe have such a system in effect, and many more have tried to implement one and abandoned the idea. Wealth tax has come up several times in the political dialog in the history of America as well. But perhaps never before has the seeming wealth imbalance been as acute. As per Wikipedia, the total wealth of the top 1% in the United States has gone from $8.4 Tr (trillion) in 1989 to $29.5 Tr in 2018, while the wealth of the bottom 50% has gone from $700B in 1989 to a negative number in 2018. According to the website Statista, in 2016 the top 10% owned 77.1% of US wealth, while the bottom 50% owned 1.2%. Within that 77% owned by the top 10%, the upper half (top 5%) owned 65% of the wealth in America. The nonlinear distribution continues with the top 1% owning 38.6% of the wealth. No matter how we look at the data, we arrive at a similar widening disparity.

Here's the rationale for a wealth tax, in the words of a finance guy:

Simply by taxing "income" the wide disparity in the wealth base cannot be levelled out, and over time will keep getting wider. But why is that? Because **wealthier citizens have not only more capital to put at risk, but also assume more risk with a large part of their capital.** Their excess capital can assume higher levels of risk without having to so much as put a scratch on their living standards. And such risk capital earns a much higher return that what ordinary folks can get – often because they have access to deals not open to everyone (did Google, Facebook or Lyft come around asking you for capital when they were fledgling startups?). Hence the need to tax the *wealth base.* Moreover, there's ample wealth "passed down the generations" to less productive heirs that are doing little to carry the torch of their entrepreneurial ancestor. Such a wealth hoard, apart from propping up the S&P 500 and pressuring bond yields, is achieving precious little. There's a strong argument that this wealth should be put to work, and a wealth tax is perhaps the only mechanism to get it moving (but moving, *to where* – this is something our proposal will address).

A side remark on Income inequality versus wealth inequality

Addressing the so-called "Warren Buffett problem" (Warren Buffett's effective tax rate is lower than his executive assistant's and it shouldn't be) by raising the marginal tax bracket on high earners will only address "income inequality" and do little to level "wealth inequality". Warren Buffett's billions in wealth (I mean, charity) will sit pat (mostly, at the Gates Foundation), and continue to grow, considering it is invested well. It will do little to level income inequality as well – and very likely annihilate an incentive for highly motivated individuals that work the hardest and deliver knock-on effects that help our economy (who gets out of bed early and rushes to work – Sam Walton's heirs? Or a Walmart regional manager?). Further, Warren Buffett could go on the (in)famous "annual salary of $1" and never face the raised marginal tax bracket.

Therefore, **solutions for income inequality do not address the issue,** *and these will be excluded from the recipe.*

Examples of wealth tax proposals on the table start taxing wealth well below $100m of wealth and have a rate of taxation that goes as high as 8%.

Wealth tax- why not?

Suppose we are sitting at a point in time where a law has been passed - and one of the existing wealth tax proposals would get implemented in a years' time. Those that sit at high levels of wealth immediately scramble to "get the wealth off their books". How? They give it away to charities they set up (like so many already have), where they essentially control how that wealth is disbursed (they were not planning to use most of it in their lifetime anyway). Even better, two such individuals team up and come to an agreement to manage each other's charities (apologies to anyone that is collecting brownie points for giving away his wealth to a friend's Foundation). And there must be other arcane ways to restructure wealth that someone in my standing is simply not allowed to know, so we will just refer to all of that as "charity".

As a consequence of such restructuring, the nation's expected "wealth tax collection" falls fabulously short (as it did in Europe), the expected public service benefits fail to materialize, and all the college education that was supposed to "become free" stays well out of reach. In response, certain edgy politicians propose yet another legislation to tighten the screws on charitable contributions (or ban them altogether) – which puts all charities in a cash crunch. Ironically, with charities not acting as charitable anymore, the very same people these wealth tax proposals were supposed to make whole are caught on the wrong side.

Is that all? No. Newer generations grow up and enter the workforce with a new mantra – there's now "less incentive" to work super hard and create wealth. A nation built on the bedrock of initiative, enterprise and risk-taking loses a fundamental driving force and becomes more like a cold, socialist country around the Arctic circle – only with no Aurora Borealis or fjords. Imagine – had this been implemented in America two centuries ago – Hugh Jackman would have gotten stuck with his Wolverine claws because "the Greatest Showman" wouldn't have existed in history.

In this backdrop, young men and women with great ideas and the will of Alexander Hamilton, but sparse resources, do a Google search on which countries do not have a wealth tax. Gradually the entire system catches on, and the ecosystem of entrepreneurship, risk taking, wealth creation – and an entire generation of Sergei Brins and Kylie Jenners – move to these countries. Wealth tax implementations come with severe tax penalties for wealthy US citizens abandoning their citizenship – but none for 21 year-olds exiting with big ideas and dreams, student loans and no tangible assets. If you're a successful entrepreneur, and you and your 21-year old daughter have a great idea for enterprise software, wouldn't you be tempted to take that idea out of the country?

Severe opponents of a wealth tax would like these to be the closing arguments, and bury any wealth tax proposal. Hence, we ask ...

Why then, at all…?

Why should we worry about a wealth tax to redistribute wealth at all? For starters, history has shown that society can only take so much economic disparity before the disadvantaged are pushed into action – threatening peace and stability. The Peasants' Revolt in Medieval England. The Bolshevik revolution in the early 20th century Russia. The Arab Springs in 2010. At the time of writing there are protests ongoing in Hong Kong for 2+ months that started on a different cue and morphed into a rebellion against costs and standards of living. About a year ago the "Yellow Vests" took to the streets in the nation known for protests throughout history. "Occupy Wall Street" (a year after Arab Springs) was more a tremor than a success – they didn't even properly make it into their main target on Wall Street – but it showed the global power of a social media-fueled rally. Perhaps in no city in America is the "bloodless rebellion" as stark as in San Francisco, where cost of housing and homelessness are at extreme points. According to a <u>Business Insider article</u>, the number of instances of 'human acts of desecration' on the streets of San Fran went from 5500 in 2011 (bad enough) to 28,000 in 2018 (beyond belief) –

"bloodless revolution" indeed, but unfortunately, not devoid of 'biological matter'.

Although there are billionaires who want to settle down on Mars, do billionaires want to live in a vacuum, surrounded by a hostile wasteland?

Addressing these issues would be timely and pertinent. But since we brought up the social angle, let us first answer …

Does reducing wealth inequality automatically increase public welfare?

The answer is no. "Wealth Inequality" has received so much popular attention of late that it is being used interchangeably with all forms of inequality, including gaps in opportunities, services, access to resources. But addressing wealth inequality does not automatically address these other gaps – it depends on the method.

To discuss methods for reducing wealth inequality we need to measure it first. We can measure wealth inequality via a measure of dispersion (say, standard deviation) of wealth among Americans, or via a measure of "skew" – the difference between the mean and the median wealth.

Consider the following measures of reducing wealth inequality, or dispersion in wealth:

1. <u>Half-a-Robinhood</u> (also known as, robbery): Impose a tax on the wealthy, but do not distribute the collection amongst the rest. That will reduce both the dispersion and the skew, and hence reduce wealth inequality, but it would do nothing to improve the lives of the people that were galvanized into voting for the proponent and sup-

posed to have benefited. (In fact, there might be a negative effect because there's less productive wealth in the hands of the rich to invest into the economy).

2. <u>Full-Robinhood</u>: Collect wealth tax and give dollar-for-dollar in handouts to the rest. Lowers wealth in the hands of the rich *and* increases wealth amongst the rest. This squeezes wealth dispersion even more and thus reduces wealth inequality to a greater extent than half-a-Robinhood. The intended beneficiaries do benefit and are able to address immediate needs with these handouts, but do not necessarily get a foundation they can build on for the future.

3. <u>This-ain't-Robinhood</u> (wealth tax): Collect wealth tax, put it in the coffers of the Federal Tax budget and pray that by some mechanism that is neither guided nor planned, the collected amount rides on the back of a dart through a jungle of tax priorities and lands right in the hands of those that need it. The reader should recognize that these are the current wealth tax proposals on the table. This can be almost as perverse as half-a-Robinhood. Is it this lack of fairness and *attributability* that billionaires are raising their voice against?

*Owing to these reasons **focusing on reducing wealth inequality via a wealth tax might simply be a misplaced goal.***

Fortunately, with some alterations, we can do better. Our proposal holds that a *Direct, Attributable and Transparent* transfer of this 'tax' can super-charge investment into programs that not only reduce wealth inequality, but also *sustain a virtuous cycle of wealth creation and growth at the other end of the spectrum.* This would serve public welfare while reducing wealth inequality, and faster. The mechanism would open up access to tools and resources to sustain and create wealth at the other end. And we think, billionaires would be willing to participate in it, maybe even with enthusiasm.

A few other points that we have considered in our proposal

- <u>Wouldn't *you* want to know where your money went?</u> It is fair to argue that many wealthy citizens are not averse to contributing to the world around – judging by the scale of initiatives they have launched. But perhaps they are not convinced in the government's ability to channel their wealth to uses they think "are right". Would a wealthy individual want to just pay a wealth tax and watch it go into an unmanaged black hole? Perhaps a certain billionaire public personality is willing to build a hospital that provides free preventive screening, but has no faith in a national healthcare system because her auntie got a taste of a year-long wait time at the NIH in the UK.

- <u>The hoarders</u>: The wealthy have loads of risk-capital – yet there are those that are "stashing it away" and not putting it 'at risk', despite banks paying hardly any interest. It was accumulated by their Grandfather's shipping company, and they don't need to take any risk to cruise through a comfortable life. How can they be given an incentive to sail into adventurous waters?

- <u>Could capital inequality be the root of wealth inequality?</u> If we were to mandate a re-distribution of wealth to the disadvantaged, should we not, in parallel, empower them with the resources and access to invest this cash flow into their ideas? Should we not encourage enterprise in this under-served segment that knows its problems better than the rest? While a direct cash handout provides for short-term needs ("get through the end of month"), a wise capital investment can build a foundation for tomorrow (and even reduce the need for such programs in future). Many other sources address the short-term, including the many traditional charities and the existing federal tax budget. There's sparse capital available for ideas coming out of anything other than "the expected entrepreneurs with a Rolodex". While many with bright minds but not much else languish in getting their ideas funded, others with a supermodel sister or a prominent dad hoodwink investors with unicorn valuations while drinking $140 bottles of tequila at work. Does any mandate to transfer wealth do justice if the intended beneficiaries do not have the chance or access necessary to give life to an idea? We think this deserves a flow of capital along with guidance. The oft-recommended *micro-loans demanding high interest and swift payback are not only inadequate, but in many cases corrosive.*

That leads us to the proposal we call ABC

We started out with a promise of something "better than wealth tax", so let us start by giving it a name – *"ABC"* (Asset-Based Contribution). It is a levy – but implementing *a levy alone is just the beginning – because it is very incomplete without clear rules and governance on how it gets deployed.* Our *ABC* proposal will address this equally important complementary piece.

Here's the summary of ABC:

A 3% (<u>variable</u>) asset-based contribution on wealth above \$1B – can be paid to the government as a "tax", but will be waived if the entire amount is invested in a certified project or a startup venture that benefits the public. The investor will own his/her proportionate stake in the project/venture, and be free to harvest any gains after 5 years. The original amount should be re-invested into another certified program/venture.

The asset-based contribution amount should not be subject to any other taxes.

The 3% contribution rate makes sense at the time of writing – but it is important that the policy be flexible to reset it. We'll discuss this in a later section.

What *ABC* would mobilize is the supply of capital available for social projects that would normally have sparse sources of funding. More on these projects/ventures later with some examples.

<u>Thoughts on implementation</u>:

Any citizen should be free to propose a project/venture to qualify for certification.

Programs would be certified by an anonymous body of reviewers that adhere to guidelines and are drawn randomly from a Board of knowledgeable citizens (much like "jury duty", and a bit like reviewing academic papers – *gratis* public service performed by members of the community).

Any project/venture that is already in existence can qualify for certification, provided it fulfills necessary criteria.

The allocation of asset-based contributions to projects/ventures would be determined by <u>an open bidding process</u> (keep it *Transparent*).

In this day and age where information technology and digital platforms can achieve a variety of unimaginable feats, we recommend getting the tech giants in one room and cleverly incentivizing them to build the platform – on their war chest of cash.

Why should the first $1B of wealth be excluded from the ABC levy?

Why should *ABC* not apply to the first $1B of wealth? Because dreaming of becoming a billionaire is a powerful engine of growth – this dream is perhaps the DNA of America's success. Any enterprising individual needs to keep the dream alive and keep striving – assured that new regulations do not impact the dream. We need as many of them as possible to maximize the chances of creating a visionary that has a monumental impact on our lives. No complaints if such visionaries from all over get drawn to the dream and leave their home countries, to create their value here, as many have.

By keeping the American dream alive, we are, in fact, benefiting more than just America. It is a confluence of the American spirit and ecosystem that gets full credit for giving birth to the visionary entrepreneurs that created many of today's global enterprises. Korean conglomerate Samsung would not have been a major player in the smartphone industry if there was no iPhone to draw 'inspiration' from 12 years ago. There wouldn't have been 'cheap handsets' driving connectivity and access across the remotest parts of emerging countries. E-commerce outside America, which is still several years, even decades behind, would not have received consideration or capital if America had not provided the formula with its one massive success story. An entire cottage industry of venture capitalists and entrepreneurs sit outside America, ready to plunk capital into ideas that are "working in America". Thus were formed ride-sharing services such as Didi Chuxing, Olacabs, Careem around the world, on the heels of Lyft and Uber (the latter, built on technology developed by Alphabet's Waymo subsidiary). Ever heard of Xing, the German version of LinkedIn? Or Mixi, the Japanese social network? Or Yandex, the Russian search engine and portal? WeChat, the substitute for WhatsApp, which is banned in China? How about just "Hollywood Bowl", a British company that brought bowling alley entertainment to the UK? All of this, without counting the global influence of American artists on global pop culture. The American dream is an energy core that drives not just America, but the whole world.

Pardon the digression - being a stock-picker specializing in companies outside America that was a topic I can discuss for hours. Back to the levy – we should ask if there were a **smaller** *ABC* levy of say 0.4% on wealth between $500m - $1B, would that kill the dream? That is at most a $2m check asked of those worth between $500 - $1B. Back-of-the-envelope math suggests that collections from this category could be a relevant fraction of the collections on the 1B+ wealth. The half-a-billionaires might even feel left out if they're not allowed to participate in certified programs (very tempted to insert a smiley here).

What about the problem of high value illiquid assets that cannot release cash of satisfy *ABC*?

If a billionaire owns assets that are simply not liquid (ie, cannot be readily turned into cash, nor can they readily pay a dividend), s/he has a problem (not every billionaire can sell shares in their publicly-listed company every day to fund a space program). A private startup, still burning through cash and developing its main product - may be valued at $4B, but there is no immediate market for its shares. The founder that owns 40% of the company is worth $1.6B, and has to make an asset-based contribution on $600m of wealth, a levy of $18m. But his annual cash compensation is only $500,00, as it is common for entrepreneurs to have most of their compensation connected to the company's share price, liquid or not. So he throws up his hands and says he cannot pay the levy. This was one of the sticky points that led to some countries in Europe shuttering their wealth tax programs.

Rather than abandon the entire system because of this "issue", the government needs to assist in creating liquidity. A solution would be a program under which banks can lend against shares of private companies as collateral. Such loans should be guaranteed by the government, much like pools of housing mortgages from Fannie Mae. Points to note:

- Since the govt is imposing a levy on a certain assessed value of the private company, the govt must believe the company has value and hence should have no problem guaranteeing a loan against that valuation.

- Bankers should not only have no problem lending, they should do so happily, at a "tight spread" (a couple of percentage points higher than the risk-free rate), given government guarantees on the loan. Even without a govt guarantee, hyped-up private companies seem to enjoy enormous credit lines right up to their failed IPO. This might even turn into a "peer-to-peer lending" party, with one billionaire CEO of a certain bank lending to other billionaires.

These loans will put some cash in the hands of the private-company owner, and remove an excuse for not being able to pay the levy. The govt-backed loans with private assets as collateral will also create some fresh new "fixed income securities", and trading, and fees - I doubt, though, that the investment banks will send a postcard thanking me for the idea.

Why does the 3% rate for *ABC* make sense? Why should the program retain the flexibility to alter it?

Our argument is based on two conflicting considerations.

(1) We want to incentivize "idle capital" – the kind sitting in the hands of non-enterprising heirs – to take on enough risk and hence earn a higher return. If these heirs can earn 5% interest from bank accounts and high-grade bonds (call it 3.5% after-taxes), they could just pay out their wealth tax without taking any real risk – and still hang on to the same level of wealth. If this rate is set too low, such as the 1% in a recent proposal, the "idle heir" can actually retain their wealth base without getting out of bed. The asset-based contribution rate should be set high enough to encourage "idle capital" to take sufficient risk on investments. We propose that the rate of levy should be = the after-tax return on risk-free assets + a risk premium (which reflects the additional return generated by the risk we want this wealth capital to

assume). Prevailing risk-free rates are ~1.5% (~1% after tax), adding to that a 2% risk premium gets us to that 3% contribution rate (as a point of reference: investors in common stocks demand an additional 3% - 8% return owing to the extra risk assumed).

(2) On the other hand, suppose we set this rate rather high, such as 8% - as recommended by a proponent who perhaps hasn't checked the interest rate in his savings account since 1980. Earning 1% per year after tax and paying an 8% levy implies a 7% attrition annually. At this rate the wealth will shrink to $(0.93)^9$ in under 9 years, by 48%. In less than 20 years it would have lost 75%. (The scientist in me is tempted to label this as – *'an 8% levy gives wealth a half-life of under 10 years'*). The possibility of such an attrition will sharply increase the incentive for 'a dodge', even spark rebellion and defeat the purpose of redirecting wealth to public welfare.

If in **normal and healthy economic times** the interest rate in a savings account becomes 5% (most of us remember that rate), i.e. 3.5% post-tax, it would be reasonable to raise the asset-based contribution rate to 5%. But we emphasize <u>normal and healthy economic times</u>. Imagine a scenario where we arrived at that 5% interest rate after an inflationary shock, the economy is in trouble and market returns are suffering – some of that billion+ wealth has now fallen below a billion, while the rest might be suffering from negative returns. Should the policy add to the injury by increasing the contribution rate, while the wealth base is shrinking?

To conclude – while the rate of contribution should vary with interest rates and the economic climate, we think it would require rather unusual conditions to justify an *ABC* rate outside the 2% to 5% range, given the considerations above.

And from the viewpoint of serving public welfare, how does the *ABC* program look ?

We have viewed the proposal from the standpoint of billionaires, as well as those that have been left out. How does *ABC* and its allocations to certified programs look from the standpoint of officials whose sole goal is public welfare? Does *ABC* improve the allocation to items of need, and make the process more *Direct, Attributable and Transparent*?

Consider an environment where *ABC* has been implemented, and a set of certified programs and ventures are on the table – phone lines open. There are two kinds of programs here – **investment programs**, that can generate a return for the contributor, and **benefit programs**, that are essentially a donation. Generally speaking, the former **lay a foundation for tomorrow**, while the latter **secure the needs of today, to get through to tomorrow.**

In listing these sample certified programs for ABC, I have drawn on proposals in the media and my experience of looking at public finance initiatives across the world. Below are some hypothetical examples – a nation full of smart people can imagine many more:

1. <u>Student loans for economically disadvantaged students</u> attending college. This is an example – students from families earning < $75,000 annually – qualify for loans that cover tuition and living expenses and have 8 years after leaving college to pay them back. The interest rates on these loans are initially priced at 3.5% (assuming Fed funds rate at 2%, this might possibly be below market). We say initially, because the final interest rates these students pay will depend on the demand for investing in these loans. Billionaires with a need to direct their asset-based contribution to a certified program will compete to lend college money to these students. The final interest rate might very well end up below 3.5%, or, perhaps, even below 2%, depending on the amount of capital competing to lend, and *these students would be the beneficiaries of the lower interest rates.* What *ABC* does is increase the supply of capital to this purpose. (Note that under the current system the students are first granted the loans at a <u>fixed rate</u>, and then some bank securitizes the pool of loans, layers their 'service fee', and sells the pool of loans as 'fixed income securities' to yield-hungry investors. These investors might very well drive the implicit yield on the loan pool to 2%, and bond traders benefit from the the rise in the "face value" of the bonds. Not the students. Shouldn't this change?)

2. <u>Affordable housing and urban development projects</u>. The billionaire can invest their asset-based contribution in US real estate requiring urban regeneration, provided they also plunk in a matching amount into redevelopment, improvement of public services, etc. Again, while there can be significant returns associated with the project, it is perhaps riskier than the student loans above. This assessment of risk versus reward will determine how much capital is drawn to it.

3. <u>Venture funding for businesses launched by members of families making less than $75,000 per year</u>. The startup should be in an approved area of public service – such as education, environment, health, consumer protection, safety, etc. The billionaire's contribution provides full working capital and guidance in exchange for, say, a 35% stake and governance. This will encourage entrepreneurship amongst a section of the population that rarely gets an opportunity to bring their ideas to the forefront. These ideas would get a fair chance and create a few more Joy Manganos. Some financial return, and in a few cases perhaps very high returns, to the billionaire are possible, but the risk-reward is very different from the prior two options.

4. <u>Childcare, job fair, and re-training for parents in need</u>. Free childcare centers, organizing job fairs and overall assistance to re-train and re-purpose parents, especially single parents. No immediate financial benefit to the billionaire, except that they have the option of getting their name out to the recipient of the assistance, and

first shot at recruiting them. The reward from this program is very different from the prior three – it is largely a public service.

5. <u>And the rest – tax refunds for low earners</u>. A certain x % of the income taxes paid by the bottom half of earners would be refunded (as per taxfoundation.org, the bottom half of earners pay less than 4% of the total income tax revenues generated). Few billionaires would probably volunteer to direct their *ABC* in this category, so any unused *ABC* that did not go to the first four categories end up here. The value of x would depend on the unused *ABC* available. The billionaire again has the option of getting their name out to the recipient, along with perhaps coupons to a large retail store they control, but there's no direct financial benefit involved unlike the first 3 options.

We will highlight again, the first three are all *investment projects,* with varying levels of risk-reward, while the last two are *benefit programs.* And this is only a 'strawman' for illustration.

The final allocation of capital to the above five projects/venture categories will depend on the following factors:

-   The set of billionaires that intend to make asset-based contributions, and the total capital thus available for allocation.

- Each contributor's "utility function" – a combination of risk-reward, preferences, needs - of the billionaire making the asset-based contribution. It could be that the least risky category of student loans is the most popular and gets rapidly taken up (to the glee of students who enjoy a lower interest rate). However, a contributor that is "late" to the process finds that all that is left to choose from is the last category of public-service programs with no financial returns, because the first three categories have already been fully funded. On the contrary, there's a contributor with a charitable mindset who prefers to build a childcare center for single parents ahead of the other options.

- The supply of proposals. In a particularly great year for America, perhaps there are no urban real estate projects – instead the only investment projects we have are the first and third options (student loans and startup ventures).

The success of the *ABC* program will also depend on there being adequate "capacity" - an adequate supply of such certified programs. Every dollar of *ABC* that is looking for a program should have a program available if we truly live in a country haunted by inequality.

A consideration on charities...

Should charities with billionaires involved be also subject to an *ABC* levy? After all, charity should begin at home, so is it too much to ask well-endowed charities to allocate 3% annually to certified programs? This may, in fact, not even change anything for these charities, if they are already doing similar work within the country. This will make the billionaire indifferent to setting up a charity versus simply making an asset-based contribution. It will also ensure that the wealth billionaires have already given away to charity continue to do their fair share for programs of public interest within our borders. We think, such charities should at least be audited for such domestic participation, and the avenue to impose an *ABC* levy left open.

Does *ABC* have something for everyone?

We set out to strike a balance in satisfying multiple parties with conflicting goals – and here's the scorecard:

- The less privileged would clearly benefit from *ABC* – with directly funded programs that let them build a foundation, while also fulfilling certain immediate needs.

- Billionaires do have to give up some of their wealth, but many are happy to re-direct their charitable efforts to fully transparent, certified programs where they have ownership and can even harvest some returns. And like any citizen, they are free to use their exceptional resources to propose excellent programs for certification.

- Those concerned about idle wealth getting hoarded are pleased because there is an incentive for the hoarder to mobilize such wealth and put it to work. The hoarders don't like getting out of bed initially, but pretty soon they overcome inertia and are on with the program, realizing that "getting on the treadmill" is a great way to "be someone better" (paraphrasing a famous line from 'As Good as it Gets'. Incidentally, the title of this book is also inspired by a line from the same movie).

- Those clamoring against wealth inequality are also pleased – *ABC* will certainly narrow the wealth gap and do much more.

- Last, but perhaps very importantly, the proposal keeps alive incentives for hard work, enterprise and initiative, and achieves the above points without denting the American dream.

ABC appears to have captured a seat as a Pareto optimal alternative. It is indeed rare to have found an alternative that satisfies everyone (that's why such an option is called the "Utopia point"), so let us explore …

Who is not happy with *ABC*? (and, lets get some rough numbers)....

W ell, there's got to be some constituents that were hoping to plow the proceeds of the wealth tax straight into the federal Tax Budget – instead now it is going to certified programs which they can't control! They were hoping to use this wealth tax "windfall" to fund *their* favorite programs and not the ones chosen through transparent bidding. The suspicious billionaire feared this all along - satisfying lobbyists, increasing government spending, and in general, "promoting bloat", rather than find ways to be lean. These people are very unhappy, even though *ABC's* certified programs are addressing some of the same focus areas that would have eaten into the federal tax budget.

US Federal tax collection has been running at a clip of $3.3 trillion per year in recent years, slated to rise to $3.6 trillion by 2020 (source: TheBalance.com). In contrast, how big is the 3% ABC levy on the 1B+ wealthholders? Let us take a crack at estimating this.

Per Wikipedia, in 2019 there are 2153 billionaires in the world, with a total wealth of $8.7 trillion. Of them, 609, or 28% are in the US. However, considering that many

Americans sit at the top of that list, a higher percentage of billionaire wealth is held by Americans. I do not have that figure, but I'm sure *Forbes* or someone can help the cause here. I would like to assume that American billionaires own half the $8.7 trillion, but the number is more likely between that 28% and 50%. If 40% of the $8.7 trillion is owned by the 609 US billionaires, we have a figure of $3.48 trillion in US billionaire wealth. Of that, since the first billion for each US billionaire is exempt from ABC's 3% levy, the base figure for the 3% levy is $3,480 B - $609 B = $2,871B.

A 3% levy on $2,871 B would raise $86B.

If 40% is not the right figure, instead it is closer to 50%, the $86B would be closer to $107B. **Either way, the 3% levy collects less than 3% of the total expected federal income tax budget of $3.6tr expected in 2020.** In a normal economy, that 3% could just come from growth and inflation, and some efficiency programs. Is that 3% collection better served in adding a small slack in the federal income tax budget? Or is it better served in the Direct, Attributable and Transparent certified programs that we laid out?

Can't satisfy everyone, and in the best Pareto optimal solutions, we wouldn't.

A word of caution...

We would caution against unintended consequences if these recommendations are cherry-picked and adopted piecemeal. For example, if the *ABC* levy is implemented, without the government guarantee on bank loans against illiquid assets owned by a billionaire, asset-rich but cash-poor billionaires fail to pay, and get away with it. Gradually, many entrepreneurs just decide to keep their company private, and the common investor in America loses out on great investments. If we just implement a flat "3% levy" because the considerations on a variable rate "are too complicated", we will create the wrong incentives if banks start paying an interest rate of 7%, or worse, rates go negative like in Germany, Switzerland or Japan. Hence, *ABC* should be treated as a complete system of interconnected ideas, - a cherry-picked subset of proposals will leave an anomaly somewhere.

You may say that I'm a dreamer....

But I can't help this thought. Perhaps we do not even need to go through a political process to establish *ABC*. Perhaps the wealthy find the idea of allocating their wealth *transparently* to programs for greater good so compelling, that they voluntarily sign-up to allocate annually a fraction of their excess wealth. Isn't that all we need?

Thank you for reading and reflecting.

66

I hope someday you'll join us

~ John Lennon, the legendary Beatles ~

Contact the author:

IDas07@gsb.columbia.edu

ON THE LIGHTER SIDE

Two economists, a consultant, and a mathematician are called on to solve a problem of global importance….

After a week of analysis, it is time to re-convene and present findings –

TWO ECONOMISTS: We had the solution in mind from Day One – we spent all our time figuring out the assumptions that would fit the solution. We have no idea what happens if we implement this, but who does? We need a bigger team.

MATHEMATICIAN: Team? Mathematicians like to work alone. Here is the theorem and here is the proof - in abstract form. It may not quite apply to this problem, but the theorem is rather elegant, and I've already sent it out for publication.

CONSULTANT: Here's a google search for solutions that have been proposed. No one has ever implemented any of these. I have a complete proposal for a series of follow-on projects that will last long enough for me to retire.

Further Reading

Manual of Political Economy. *VILFREDO PARETO. 1906*

How Aid to the Poor Is Also an Investment *JARED BERNSTEIN. MARCH 2014*

We are businessmen in the 1%. It's time to increase taxes on us. *THE PATRIOTIC MILLIONAIRES. OCT 2019*

Taxing the Rich Is an Idea Whose Time Has Come — and Gone *STEPHEN MINN (BLOOMBERG OPINION). JAN 2019*

A Wealth Tax Might Be Easier to Implement than You Think *STEVE WAMHOFF (INSTITUTE ON TAXATION AND ECONOMIC POLICY). JULY 2019*

Why Europe Axed Its Wealth Taxes. *CHRIS EDWARDS (CATO INSTITUTE). MARCH 2019.*

Normal-boundary intersection: A new method for generating the Pareto surface in nonlinear multicriteria optimization problems. *I Das, JE Dennis. SIAM journal on Optimization 8 (3), 631-657. 1998.*